# THE GREAT BIRD OF LOVE

# THE GREAT BIRD
# OF LOVE

POEMS BY

PAUL ZIMMER

UNIVERSITY OF ILLINOIS PRESS

URBANA AND CHICAGO

Manufactured in the United States of America
P   5   4   3   2

*This book is printed on acid-free paper.*

Library of Congress Cataloging-in-Publication Data

Zimmer, Paul.
    The great bird of love : poems / by Paul Zimmer.
       p. cm. — (National poetry series)
      ISBN 0-252-06060-1 (alk. paper)
      I. Title. II. Series.
    PS3576.I47G74 1989
    811'.54 — dc19               88-23530
                                      CIP

Digitally reprinted from the second paperback printing

## ACKNOWLEDGMENTS

Certain of these poems have appeared in the following magazines, some in slightly altered forms. The author and publisher wish to express their grateful acknowledgments to:

*Black Warrior Review, Chariton Review, Denver Quarterly, Fine Madness, Memphis State Review, New Letters, Open Places, Paintbrush, Poetry Northwest, Poetry Now, Poetry Wales, Sierra Madre Review, Small Towner, Swallow's Tale, Three Rivers Poetry Journal,* and *Yankee.*

The following poems appeared in the *Georgia Review:* "Zimmer to His Students" and "Zimmer Closes His Family Home."

The following poems appeared in the *Gettysburg Review:* "The Origins of Love" and "How Zimmer Will Be Reborn."

The author and publisher also wish to thank the following presses for permission to reprint poems that previously appeared in chapbooks or anthologies:

Ampersand Press, for permission to reprint the following poems from *Live with Animals:* "Lessons from the History of Bears," "The Sounds of Magpie," "How Birds Should Die," "Doing Business with Animals," and "The Great Bird of Love";

Slow Loris Press, for permission to reprint the following poem from *The Ancient Wars:* "Zimmer Ponders His Life in Books";

Bradbury Press, for permission to reprint the following poem, which originally appeared in their anthology, *Strings: A Gathering of Family Poems,* edited by Paul Janeczko: "Missing the Children";

The University Press of New England, for permission to reprint the following poems, which originally appeared in their anthology, *The Breadloaf Anthology of Contemporary American Poetry,* edited by Robert Pack, Sydney Lea, and Jay Parini: "The Place" and "The Great Bird of Love."

The author also wishes to acknowledge with gratitude the National Endowment for the Arts for a Writing Fellowship in 1984 and the Academy and Institute of American Arts and Letters for an Award in Literature in 1985. Both of these honors were highly beneficial to the completion of the poems in this book.

# The National Poetry Series

The National Poetry Series was established in 1978 to publish five collections of poetry annually through five participating publishers. The manuscripts are selected by five poets of national reputation. Publication is funded by James A. Michener, Edward J. Piszek, The Copernicus Society of America, The Lannan Foundation, and the five publishers—E. P. Dutton, Graywolf Press, the Atlantic Monthly Press, Persea Books, and the University of Illinois Press.

1988

*After We Lost Our Way* by David Mura
Selected by Gerald Stern. E. P. Dutton

*Black Wings* by Len Roberts
Selected by Sharon Olds. Persea Books

*The Great Bird of Love* by Paul Zimmer
Selected by William Stafford. University of Illinois Press

*Green the Witch Hazel Wood* by Emily Heistand
Selected by Jorie Graham. Graywolf Press

*Constant Mercy* by Lee Upton
Selected by James Tate. Atlantic Monthly Press

*to*

*Stan and Marie Felver,*
*Jean Burden,*
*John McGowan,*
*Fred Hetzel,*

*who helped the turtle cross the road*
*many years ago,*

*and, as always,*
*to my dearest loves,*
*Suzanne, Justine,*
*Erik, Margaret,*
*and Aaron Paul*

# CONTENTS

# PART 1

---

*A long train of diseases is likewise entailed upon the
studies of poets, philologers, divines, and in time all
writers and the other retainers to learning who are chiefly
employed in the functions of the mind. Above all, it goes
hardest with the poets, who, by reason of the fantastic
ideas always present in their minds both night and day,
are timorous, morose, and very lean, as their aspects
testify.*

—Ramazzini, an Italian physician, 1700
from his book on occupational diseases

# THE FLOWERING

When the decision was made
There was no turning back.
Before I was Zimmer
My face unclutched and
Warily spread its petals
Until I was all invitation
And unsullied delight.

How I became Zimmer
Does not matter now;
It is an old story of
Time and hard weather
Not to be told again.

Instead I try to recall
Things beyond memory,
How first light slid into
My eyes and each thing
That I saw came to me
As if created
Expressly for my wonder.

# THE GREAT PEACE

Zimmer marched in the winters of world war,
Through long newsreels of dismal snow and puddles,
Into an August night in '45 when peace came.
He rose with his family, turned on the lights,
Sat in the kitchen, drinking sweetened ice tea,
Listening to car horns, church bells and whistles,
Trying to feel relief. The moon came up over
The backyard, ripening out in all directions,
Sky was streaked with the juice of its fullness.
Beyond it, Zimmer knew, Japanese cities were exploded,
Europe was burned to the ground, millions had died
Before their time. He knew what he should be feeling,
And he knew what he felt. He was eleven years old,
It was summer, the moon made him feel strange,
The rest of his life was on its way.

# WOUNDS

When I think of men alone
I remember how the big war ended
In '45 and there was baseball in
Our town again. The American Legion
Brought veterans from hospitals,
Lined them up in wheel chairs
Just behind the backstop screen.
All of us gazed with pride,
Then I saw one weeping beneath
The stands, was puzzled by this,
But felt sorry and forgave him.

I recall my own dispensable days
When sergeants told me if I was
Hit in combat to roll away
So others could get through,
Not to make noise nor wave
My arms too much for medics lest
I draw fire upon the company.

Now when I walk at night
I see helicopters flap in
Over the city, swoop down
And deliver special cases
To the veterans' hospital.
No matter the hour I rise
I can look out my window and see
Lights burning and throbbing in
That leaden, aseptic building.

# BECAUSE OF DUTIES, ZIMMER
# HAD FORGOTTEN THE FOREST

Now I see the moon rise like primitive memory
And think of solitary times, how crickets etch
Themselves into an evening like this. I watch
The humbling process of darkness begin in trees,
Their great canopies begin to grow the stars.
I do not wish to dwell upon this splendor;
I build fire and back their glister away with my glare.

I gaze at flames and recall the ferocity of bombs,
Distant towers in dawn light, the countdown until
There are no more numbers, then the flash
And deadly roll of the shock wave,
Blinded animals calling, shacks and bushes burning.

I have no comfort until new light softens my fire
And dawn begins to piece itself through leaves.
Then I recall that burning wood is delicate kinship,
That no matter what we do to trees they love
Us to the end, stroking our bones with root tips,
Topping the markers to purify our graves.

# THE DREAM OF MY SECOND CONSCRIPTION

The images form with unendurable sadness,
You and the children, helpless in despair,
As I wave goodbye from a troop bus.
How could a dream show more of loss?
My children, who grow away from me
In their lives, weep in this dream
For need of me. It is almost more
Than I can bear, that I would
Go again and not be with you,
That I would stand in freezing rain
And be assured of my inhumanity,
That I would go again to be
Taught the insult of how to kill.
Yet how could a dream so terrible
Show more of love? This is an illusion
So fraught with calamity that,
Were I to waken and not find you
Here beside me, surely I would die.

*for Suzanne*

# THE ORIGINS OF LOVE

The first time I saw her, light was falling,
Air was rich like the last days of autumn.
Despite her dazzle and warmth, I was melancholy,
As I have always been in the presence of beauty.

From then on I tried every day to be decent.
When I was crass, her lovely shoulders
Drooped like finished tulips in the garden.
I did not want to wait, and yet I waited
As I had never done before, and surely
In time the delicate snows began to fall.

So the glory of my restraint inspired me.
I became eloquent, attentive, civilized.
Times I had to say goodbye to her became
The greatest burdens of my onerous life.

Although she gave me no reason to doubt,
I was constantly afraid. I thought perhaps
A god might come and take her from me.
Somehow it pleased me that others admired her,
Yet it made my knuckles
Turn white like worried children.

# THE ELEMENTS OF ZIMMER

My head is
In the great fire
That leaps from
A faulty water heater,
Rams into my ears
And bellows, "Womb!"
My eyebrows gone,
Crew cut down to stubs,
In the pilot light's flicker
I dance.

The ground fractures and moans,
Dust begins to jitter in the rugs,
Light bulbs sway on their chords.
Outside squirrels fall from trees,
Dogs brace their legs and howl.
Inside my cells fly apart
And then slam together again.

Wind comes up the hills
Late in the year,
Hisses through bare saplings,
Making them bow and tangle
Their branches;
It breaks dawn into pieces and
Spatters my glasses with rain.

In the long days
Rain counts itself
From tips of leaves,
Seeks into my heart,
Makes my bones brace
And groan upon each other.
From low, dank clouds
That soak my spirit,
Rain remembers me.

# TWO DRINKING SONGS

*1. Zimmer Repudiates Beer*

It is an idiot's way to die,
Therefore when you next see me
I will look like a cactus needle
Sans body, liquid and weight,
But keen enough to make you pay.
No more will I raise the glass
And swallow till I see the froth.
I swear by the Muse that I will
Cease this slaughtering of brain cells,
Will no longer build this stomach
Brick by brick and glass by glass
Until the lights grow dim.
Though in summer it cools me
And in winter it warms my soul,
I herewith deny this perfection.

*2. Zimmer Resisting Temperance*

Some people view life as food served
By a psychopath. They do not trust it.
But Zimmer expects always to be happy.
Puzzled by melancholy, he pours a reward
And loves this world relentlessly.

Years ago he saw a snake suck light from
A frog's eyes. Now with his drink in hand,
He swallows and feels his own brain implode,
The vessels in his nose begin to glow.

Each day he plans to end up squatting like
Mahatma Gandhi with a glass of unsweetened tea.
He wishes he looked like a Rouault Christ.
But who says Zimmer should not compensate himself?
Though worn out at both ends,
He regards his happy middle,
His gilded eyes in the mirror.

Someday he may fall face down
In the puke of his own buoyancy,
But while the world and his body
Are breaking down,
Zimmer will hold his glass up.

# ZIMMER SENSES SOMETHING
## AT HIS WINDOW

Something came to my window last night:
Enormous footprints in the dew,
Broken circles of the spider's web,
Hair mats in berry bushes,
Drool stains on the windowsill,
Piles of steaming turds.
Something looked in when I couldn't look out.

Along roadways there are damage reports:
Throttled chickens, sundered dogs,
Uprooted trees, shattered pottery.
Something got into a barn and set it afire.
The evidence leads down the road
Up the pathway to my window.
On the sash there are claw marks.

Will it remember what it saw?
Will it come again?
Should I try somehow to improve myself?

## ZIMMER SEES IMBELLIS, THE BULLY,
## RISE FROM THE WATER

Brothers and sisters, I have seen the enemy.
I couldn't explain sudden boilings of surface,
Small fish leaping as the boat rocked
In the frigid waters of autumn,
The huge, refracted shadow in the water,
Plucking and snapping at my deep lines.

Suddenly there was lepered skunk
On the wind—and then I felt
His spleeny gaze on me, saw that
Half-mortified son-of-a-bitch
Sneaking and sliding on the shore,
All hideous angles, ruddy flesh,
His eyes streaming like infections.
God knows what had dredged him
Up from the bottom.

When he knew that I had seen him,
He hacked and stewed,
Snapping off awesome obscenities.
As I made for shore he circled
And growled, showing his mossy teeth.
I swiped at him with my blade,
Commenced to bellowing myself.

Oh we were something under that
Laden sky, sniffing rags and blood!
We spent the whole day in a lather,
Feinting and flaring at each other.
At dusk we both retreated, mumbling,
Flinging threats over our shoulders.

Brothers and sisters, I have met Imbellis.
Everyday he ruts and strikes flint
In our dry forests, shits in the waters
Of our lakes and stalks our borders.
We can do nothing but stand together.

# THE ORIGINS OF HUMOR

Once I went fishing with Cecil and Rollo.
Imbellis harassed us, raising storms
And slashing lightning down upon us,
He rammed the wind into our faces.
We were very frightened but,
Knowing that this pleased Imbellis,
We sang songs to hide our terror.

Imbellis lives in slime and morbidity,
Music is a thing he cannot suffer.
In exasperation he rose to the surface
Where we were laying for him, and when
His unseemly head bobbed up beside our boat
We bashed it with the broad side of an oar.

From then on Imbellis has believed
The world is flat, his only foods
Have been flounder and skate,
His brains are like the splatter
That gulls make on the rocks.

# ZIMMER REMEMBERS RELIGION

I wanted God to come down like an anvil
Through the fan vaulting of the chancel,
To smash the lofted chalice, precious blood
Dousing the upraised face of Father Animus.
I wanted tangible relics—bones, teeth, splinters,
Confirmed reports of prophets in the county,
The sky and sea each day to open and slam shut,
Sun veering, mountains rolling to bury Imbellis.
I wanted holy and powerful signs,
Instead, the mystic drone of Father Animus,
Waft of noxious incense in the nave,
Sermons full of platitude and caveat,
A feckless Host no more than a symbol,
Self-righteous glad-handing in vestibules.

Despite all plumage and posture, I say
Still that God is in mud and corruption.
He made this world and He is of it all:
Piddle of flies, grit between one's teeth.
He nestles not only in flutings and flower cups,
But he is in scum, envy, dry rot, invective,
He is utmost kindness, yet bewildering neglect.

# ZIMMERIUS VILISSIMUS

If I had been consulted,
This would have been a prodigious
Bird of multi-colored plumage
With a call like a freight train.
At sight of its angry, massive
Tracks in the snow, man and beast
Would have dithered with fear.
But indeed and shamefully,
It is a tiny, piss-colored bird
(formerly called a paltry tyrannulet)
Inhabiting thickets in Panama,
It hops nervously around with
Its tail half-cocked, shrieking,
Peee-yip, peee-yip, peee-yip!

# OLD WOODPECKER

In the end his tiny eyes won't focus.
Punchy, his snap gone, he spends his
Time banging on gutters and drain pipes.
He begins to slurr and churrrr,
His breath descending in a rattle,
He tells endless stories of old trees
Taken, but he has absorbed one too many
Hardwoods to his noggin, his brain
Is pudding. For the rest of his time
He will undulate around, patronized,
Spunky but sweet, remembering only
Nests of teeming carpenter ants,
Consenting grubs under flaps of bark,
The days when he was a contender
Amongst the great woods of his life.

# LESSONS FROM THE HISTORY
# OF BEARS

The moon rolled down the low branch
And dipped itself into the bear's vision;
Bear grew honey-eyed and torpid,
Scarcely made its way back to
The hollow before it fell
Into deepest slumber. No matter
How much the stars fussed,
They could not pry open its eyes.
Even the sun took a turn,
But bear belonged to the moon.
It dreamt of sweet light,
A syrup as radiant as fox fire,
It did not dream of us.
When the bear thinks,
It does not think of us.
Even if we slaughter it,
Eat its meat, wear its coat,
We cannot become the bear.
Though bear is greater
Than we are, it does
Not wish to harm us.
Now the bear is waking up,
The moon releases its hold.
Bear mumbles and farts,
Scratches its navel.
Even after long dreaming
It knows more than we know.
If we think of water, earth,
Fire or wind, the bear
Is wiser than we are.

This is a difficult lesson,
But we cannot dwell on it,
Dare not let it perturb us.
If we think of numbers,
God, words, the universe,
Bear knows more than we know.

# THE SOUNDS OF MAGPIE

Nobody ever owned magpie,
But now he is down in the berm.
His friends hold raucous wake
Above him before they drift away.
Magpie needs no undertaker,
Has always been dressed for the end.

Magpie attempted to live a good life,
Built well and saved bright things he loved.
He tried speaking gently to his children,
But forever ended saying, raw-raw-raw!

He loved his mate and chased with her,
Kissed her with a clack when they met;
As they made love he'd go, aw-aw-aw!

Magpie would get sick with the drink;
He picked dead flesh off an old cow's back,
Flew to a tree and threw up, aarrgh!

When magpie was young he said, now-now-now!
When he grew old he gargled with glass,
Ground his beak and said, fuck you, fuck you!

Magpie grew quiet, knew something was up,
He let the young birds chatter and chase.
One day he went to feed on the road;
When he got smacked he said, oof!

# THE NEWS OF THE DAY

The voice of our leaders
is the sound of water rising,
cruelty of fire discovering tinder,
thud of boulders after a long fall.

The voice of Zimmer
is the hiss of smoke from sapwood,
fidget of mice in weeds,
any rain that falls on the roof.

This is the news of the day:
ill winds drubbing the government,
rebellions pulverized in far countries,
threats and howling at the borders,
armies lacing up for war.

This is the news of Zimmer:
his breakfast egg was spotted,
today his bowels were airy,
a bed spring creaked as he slept,
three of his words fell into place.

# ZIMMER AND THE AGE
# OF ZEPPELINS

There was the faint sound
Of a piano playing ragtime
And then an abrupt eclipse.
Zimmer looked up and saw the zeppelin
Like a giant okra ponderously
Sliding over trees and rooftops,
Its girders creaking, echoing.

It took all day to pass over
As the sound of idle laughter
Drifted down from the promenade
And Zimmer heard tinkle of
Ice and glasses from the lounge.
At dusk he watched its fins
Cross over into the night.

It had been such an awesome day
That Zimmer could not comprehend
A sudden astonishing fireball
And thunder over the horizon,
The end of the age of zeppelins.

He ran to see the great craft
Roaring in its own air and fire,
Bodies dropping like blackened tentworms
From a torched nest and then
The whole thing down in a blazing heap,
Cries of the injured amongst the debris,
The old moon sailing on above the agony.

# THE OLD TRAINS AT NIGHT

In the forties and fifties
It seemed like every time trains
Hauled out of town at night,
They rolled into my flawless sleep.
Awake, I loved to watch them come in
Like big dogs breathing hard,
Grinding their teeth at the stations.
Then the first diesels came through,
Piddling on crossties and smelling of crap.
The damned things bred like dingy rabbits
Till by 1960 all the real trains were scrap.
Now the world belongs to bloodless bastards
Who tell us all the steam trains are gone.

But on rainy nights I hear them
Mope around, mumbling to themselves,
Slipping on glazed rails and belching.
I wake to hear them hooting at
Each other over the forlorn distances
And I start pulling for them, too.

They were finest in winter when
They showed what they could do,
Slamming their way through huge drifts,
Chests heaving, great hearts pounding.

But they ran best on moonlight.
Heaving out steam to secret wildflowers,
They slid through fox fire and hauled
Themselves panting into our dreams.

*for Gary Gildner*

# YELLOW SONNET

Zimmer no longer wishes to write
About the dimming of his lights,
Recounting all his small terrors.
Instead he tells of brilliance,
Walking home from first grade
In springtime, light descending
To hold itself and dazzle him
In an outburst of dandelions.
It was then he learned that
He would always love yellow,
Its warm dust on his knuckles,
The memory of gathering pieces
To carry home in his lunch pail
As a love gift for his mother.

# PART 2

---

*Keep your eyes on the fellow at the piano.*
*The sparrow. He don't know nothing,*
*but just keep your eyes on him*
*and we'll all be together*
*on what's going down.*

—Count Basie

# SITTING WITH LESTER YOUNG

Dusk must become your light
If you want to see Lester Young.
So Zimmer sits beside him at
His window in the Alvin Hotel.
Pres is blue beyond redemption.
His tenor idle on the table,
He looks down at the street,
Drinking his gin and port.
Buildings slice the last light
From the day. If Pres could
Shuffle into a club again like
A wounded animal, he would
Blow his ultimate melancholy,
But nights belong to others now.
Zimmer can only watch Pres
In the half light of his sadness,
Old whispers slipping around,
Words into melodies,
As holy silence means the most.

*for Michael S. Harper*

# PRESERVED BY MUSIC

Rain fell all day upon our words.
Our heads, leering persimmons,
Bobbed in the rank air,
Little mouths unpuckered to say,
"Pay," "reject," "yes," "hurry!"
Tongues leapt and struck as snakes
And we were poisoned by language,
Certain we would perish unrelieved
Amidst rancor and ghastly sound.

That evening musicians entertained:
Five players on saxophone,
Trumpet, drums, bass, guitar.
I was clamped shut, brooding in dankness,
But as the music angled and turned
At last I sighed like an oyster opening.

How could I continue without music?
Notes meshing like gears of bird flocks,
Powerful, fluid, wheeling and turning
Into grand ascents, sudden plungings,
They warmed pores in the ceiling,
Cold cracks between floor boards,
Nuzzled the chambers of our ears
And mingled with my spirit.

My mind slipped from its roost,
Moved off to some distant place
Where judgement is not required,
Where ferns stroke and assuage
My eyes and I feel strength in
The long marriage of trees to wind,

Where absolute clouds upheave
In the breaks and music resides,
Filling silences with glory.

*for John Engels*

# ZIMMER PONDERS HIS
# LIFE IN BOOKS

Suddenly the books fly in
Under reckless skies,
Swirling and flapping,
The inscrutable, difficult,
Excellent, insipid, insane,
As a flock of alarmed crows
Yawking and spattering.

The sky fills, then breaks,
And books wheel into a dive
Through roll and pitch of day.
Then they slump down to sit
In the trees and brood,
Pecking their lice in the rain.
But even in this heavy weather,
In midst of their complaints,
I remember their sunlit times
And how they always come back
On the great days of my life.

# THE POETS' STRIKE

On the stroke of this midnight
Let us cover our typewriters,
Throw down all pens and papers,
Build kindling fires in oil drums.
Let there be no more poems,
Not one more metaphor nor image,
No loose nor strict iambics,
No passion, anger, laughter.
Let no one cheat nor scab,
No furtive peeks in notebooks,
No secret scribbling in closets,
Let us dwell together in a void
Removed from beauty and truth.

Then let us see what will happen,
How many trees will blight,
How earth will wobble and fracture,
Words loosen and fall from dictionaries.
People will move through
Life like worms swallowing
And excreting their tedious passage.
They will beg us for one crippled line,
One near rhyme, one feeble dream,
And they will be so sorry
They will pay and pay and pay.

*for Rod Jellema*

# ZIMMER TO HIS STUDENTS

Sometimes when you lie on your back
In an open field and gaze
Up at the sky, you imagine
It is a blank piece of paper.
Your terror rises and you fear
You will plunge out into the vast,
Blue void forever. Then you will
Find that your body yearns
To sink roots, that you can
Save yourself only by clutching
The constant tufts of grass.

Almost as much as my sins,
I detest poems about poetry;
But, my dear friends, we must
Do things to save ourselves!
Thousands of us, at this moment,
Are fearing death by disregard.
Let me counsel you.

Pay attention to that which you take
For granted. Poetry comes to you
Like puberty—fervent, perplexing,
Unexpected, before you know what
Is happening. It is a humbling process,
Leading to knowledge that can preserve you.

# ZIMMER SOUTH

Always when I come to a new place
I wish that I had been born to it,
Grown up in its gardens and houses,
To have sat upon its stoops, learned
The angles of the sun and moon,
Grown in my love more naturally.

Here so many birds hang on through winter,
Singing their curious songs to the chill;
Come spring the stars hold forth in
Bushes and hardwoods, pine trees
Scour the blue under impeccable sun.

Some mornings, like a daisy, I rise smiling,
Feel the liquids oozing up the stack
Of my vertebrae, my cells splitting,
Gaining strength. With my knees locked
I lift the great bud of my head
To the sun and open wide.

But arriving South in my middle years,
Sometimes the storms roll over
To slide into my forehead.
Grasses are flattened, trees tested,
Red clay folds into my brain,
My face is awash with misgivings,
Joints rust like ancient locks
And I know there is no escape.

But then the clouds pass on again,
And I am glad to be on earth
In the South, pacing myself,

Pacing sun with darting birds
Under trees and blooming stars.
I sit again, learning a place,
Learning myself. How fortunate that
I have wasted my life in such a way,
That I have come to another new place,
Having nothing rich, but some things rare.

# MISSING THE CHILDREN

Yesterday my children left for college.
I exhausted myself with garden work.
Today I wake up feeling gnawed and sore;
I think of the baby cardinal,
Feathers askew, unwieldy in innocence,
It had fallen into my mulch hole
And I sought to help by lifting
It out on the tip of my shovel.
Promptly it ran from me into
The dog pen where it was mauled.
I sat on a stump and breathed hard
While its mother circled and shrieked.
She spent the whole day calling
And searching for her child.

I wish I had been born
Less clumsy to this world.
I think of my cabin so far away.
Because of spring it is trying
To become a poem. I feel it rise
Gracefully on ferns that tilt it to sun.
Around it saplings lift their leaves
Into the canopy of my brain. If I were
There I would thin them like a harsh god,
Arranging sky between their trunks.
The cabin is sweetened by cardinal's song.
As it unbinds from winter, groans and sighs
Upon its footers, it wonders, where is Zimmer?
But I am far away, searching the rooms
Of my house, looking for my children.

# THE RITUAL

As my father had done with me,
Once when my infant son
Woke crying from his sleep,
I carried him out to the yard
To show him the full moon
Rising branch by branch through
The trees, a vision strong enough
To settle him.
                    "Moon!" I said,
"Moon!"
                He was dazzled,
Struggled with the word until
He croaked, "Moo, moo!"

Next day when I came home
From work I went to his crib.
He was playing with his toes,
Brightened when he saw me.
"Moo!" he said, the memory
Rising behind his eyes, "Moo!"
Our first secret together,
An ancient confidence he has kept
To share now with his own son.

                *for Aaron Paul Zimmer*
                *May 14, 1987*

# ZIMMER NORTH

Snow rushes at me, a huge dismal spectre
Over the prairie from fifty miles away,
And no matter which way I turn, I fail
To avoid it, violent and cruel it tracks me
Down, grinding off a layer of my skin.

My lungs begin to fear the cold,
Fingers ache; another degree or two
Less and my heart will tighten into
A crimson fist. Not even the delicate
Hexagons of snow on my scarf console me.

I begin to remember how easy it was
To loath failure, how when I was young
I would come out of cold into taverns
And old men would turn to me, wailing
Their misfortunes and restrictions.

But having spent so much time watching
Snow rush in and wishing to do what
I thought I wanted to do, now I begin to
Comprehend the bitter coldness of old men,
Who are unable even to recall what
It was they had longed to do.

# TREES WRITING POEMS

It begins with mumbling in the roots,
Then words begin to smell verdant;
They slide up thin cords inside
The trunks and outside, rising
Through grooves in the bark
Into the balance of branches,
The flawless placement of leaves,
Spraying rainbows into the sunlight.
Most of the time this is wasted on us.
The trees perform this miracle while
We proceed in numbness with our duties,
But when we hear it to perfection,
A distant rhythmic dividing of cells,
It is what keeps us alive and well.

*for Stan Lindberg*

# PART 3

---

*AN ZIMMERN*

*Die Linien des Lebens sind verschieden*
*Wie Wege sind, und wie der Berge Gränzen.*
*Was hier wir sind, kan dort ein Gott ergänzen*
*Mit Harmonien und ewigem Lohn und Frieden.*

—Friedrich Hölderlin

TO ZIMMER

The lines of life are various; they diverge and cease
Like footpaths and the mountains' utmost ends.
What here we are, elsewhere a God amends
With harmonies, eternal recompense and peace.

—translated by Michael Hamburger

# WINTER

My mother sits alone
In the half light.
Out her window
Streetlamps chill
In the distance,
Snow begins to flitter
Through their light.
I come to hold
Her hand, to sit
With the shadows
In her room.
I am born and dead
In an instant.

## FOR L. C. Z., 1903–1986

I look out this high window
Which has given me such peace,
See only canopies of trees,
The sun side of leaves,
Shadows of nesting birds.

It makes me remember
That some native people
Did not bury their dead,
But raised them into treetops,
Trussing them into the sky.

I have always tried to be
Stalwart about death,
But at my mother's burial,
I looked back from
The departing limousine,
Saw her casket resting
On rails above the grave
As the sky hardened and closed.

# HOW BIRDS SHOULD DIE

Not like hailstones
ricocheting off concrete
nor vaporized through
jets nor drubbed
against windshields
not in flocks
plunged down into
cold sea by
sudden weather no
please no but
like stricken cherubim
spreading on winds
their tiny engines
suddenly taken out
by small pains
they sigh and
float down on
sunlit updrafts
drifting through treetops
to tumble gently
onto the moss

# ZIMMER'S INSOMNIA

Zimmer is cursed with consciousness.
There are no lids on his eyes.
Each night they burn like fanned coals,
All day give off a slate-colored smoke.

His brain pulsates like a clam in its shell,
Blood stream is full of nymphs and crustacea
That flutter at the walls of his veins.

He wants to rake his body like a dog,
But his wife slumbers sweetly at his side.
He does not wish to share his malediction.
Thus he walks alone the borders of consciousness,
Crosses fuming waters to the island of fierce dreams.

This is where the strange things live;
Animals of exhaustion, manatees and sloths,
Also the creatures of sting and laceration;
This is where they howl, where threats
Mean most and transgressions are most fearful;
This is where cold blood is shed
And final decisions are made.

# HOW ZIMMER WILL
# BE REBORN

Make it an ancient rookery,
A crumbling abbey in York,
A place where God's old slaves,
Cistercians, still dwell in
The spirit of dingy birds.

Make it a grizzled sky
Rolling over broken walls.
Make the air chill and wet,
Desire for warmth overwhelming.

Despite the outrage
Of righteous flocks
I will begin to claw my
Way up the worn stones
Toward a reechy nest
Tucked into a cranny.

When the mother rook
Goes to forage I will
Slip into the pocket
Of moldy leaves and sticks,
Snuggle down amongst
Warm, ticking eggs.

When she returns I will
Listen to her tender croaks,
Feel myself being coaxed out
By the song of woman,
The desire to come forth

Overwhelming, to rise,
Strutting and screeching
At anything that moves,
Guarding my few square yards.

# THE FARMS

I had always wondered what would last,
Surely not governments, monuments, pictures, songs.
At my cabin each day I looked out and grew
Accustomed to the farms in all directions.
But one day out walking I looked up
As light rose and fell upon a field of
Ripened oats: I heard cows groan with
Their milk, swine sigh, sheep ruminate,
Bees nuzzle and cross the blossoms.
It seemed a huge, golden door had
Opened and shut, fields flapped into
Their places like great birds before my eyes.
I knew they had always endured, holding
Despite rain, drought, wind, snow,
And in their renewal even fire would end.

# ZIMMER CLOSES HIS
# FAMILY HOME

How quickly old times empty,
Load after load, fifty years
Hauled out in a day until
Each corner has been violated.

This is the beginning of
A new kind of loneliness.
Now Zimmer has no other home
Except his own. Sometimes
It seems to him that home
Is the simple space around
His body, perhaps his very skin
As he gazes at the moon,
Hoping for a little warmth.

It is small comfort to know
That he will have to bring these
Ancient memories and pieces
Together again, put them back
Where they belong in the old house
Before he turns away to die.

It is wearisome to realize
That home is not where he goes,
But where he comes from.

# THE TENTH CIRCLE

*"More than three (3) health emergency calls
in one month from apartment to switchboard
shall be conclusive evidence to landlord that
occupant is not capable of independent living.
Landlord can then have tenant moved to such
health care facility as available."*

Dear Dad,

Do not fall for the third time,
Or if you do, tell no one.
Hunch over your agony and
Make it your ultimate secret.
You have done this before.
Shrug, tell a joke, go on.
If an ambulance slips up
Quietly to the back door
Do not get on. They mean to
Take you to the tenth circle
Where everyone is turned in
One direction, piled like cordwood
Inside the cranium of Satan
So that only the light of
Television shines in their eyes.
Dad, call if you need help,
But do not let them take you
Easily to this place where          .
They keep the motor idling
On the long black car, where if
Someone cries out in the night
Only the janitor comes.

                    Love,
                    Paul

# DOING BUSINESS WITH ANIMALS

*Not one is respectable or industrious*
*over the whole earth*

—Walt Whitman

Weary of unflagging pitch,
Of pitiless men and women
Trying to dazzle me with goods,
Now I will turn and live with animals.

If I want to purchase beads
I will see the magpie.
If I want to purchase pearls
I will see the oyster.

I will visit the bear
If I want to buy sleep.
I will visit the mink
If I want to buy sex.

If I want to have poison
The rattlesnake has it,
If I want to have children
The rabbit has many.

I will go to the hogfish
And he will sell me time.
I will go to the vulture
And he will sell me death.

# ZIMMER'S CORNER

From the Care Home Zimmer's father writes,
"I eat and sleep well, the food is good."
On the back of a snapshot he inscribes,
"Back of the old house before we sold it,"
The image of Zimmer and his grown son,
Their arms around each other's shoulders
As they stand and smile in the corner
Between the breakfast room and house.

Zimmer thinks of other family photos
Taken in this place, his father holding
Him the day he came home from being born,
Snaps of Zimmer playing in his sandbox,
Practicing his awkward baseball swing,
His first communion and graduations,
With his wife on the day of their wedding.

Now Zimmer's heart freezes into bitter,
Magenta stone when it comes to him that
He will never stand in that place again.
Years from now others will attend
That corner and, sensing their violations,
A lingering spirit from these common events,
Say to themselves in wonder and sadness,
"This must have been Zimmer's corner."

# THE EXPLANATION

Before his last fires were dowsed,
Before the irreversible stillness,
My father stormed against equivocation,
Heaving against tubes and wires
Until they had to bind him down.

The doctors asked for explanation.
He called for pencil and paper,
Angrily scribbled for a moment,
Then wrote in his clearest,
Most commanding hand, "I am dead."

# WINTER TREES

To watch snow sift into the woods is to
Feel yourself growing gently toward death.
Yet it is trees that teach us how to live.
In some places a person can exist
For many years without seeing a tree.
That must be the way of anger and despair.
Better to have the constant example
Of their patience and perfection,
To witness their blossoming and decay,
Watch snow resolve itself through branches,
Gathering softly at the nodes and shag.
Better to somehow join them and become
Part of the last stand in the world.

*for Jan Susina*

# IN THE COLD

Empty boxcars square the bitter air,
Snow mounts on their silent rooftops.
Small birds mass and veer to the south,
Geese connect their lines and withdraw.

This is the season of intimidation,
Both parents gone within months.
Weather cannot be more absolute than this.

A rabbit grows tense in the field,
Becoming the ultimate listener.
Branches gently stroke the drifts,
Shadows fasten under the grass,
But rabbit is going to stick it out.

Then spring comes and snow withdraws
Into itself, birds return and sprinkle
Down through branches of the trees.
I walk under the tempering buds
And look for childhood, turning up
Flat rocks and easing them
Back onto their dank fecundity.

Suddenly the boxcars jerk and landscape
Goes bang like a smoke stack falling;
Wheels are groaning again, easing over
Damp ties through the thawing grids
Of the towns, the land is cleaved in two,
Held apart until it empties of the train.

# THE PLACE

Once in your life you pass
Through a place so pure
It becomes tainted even
By your regard, a space
Of trees and air where
Dusk comes as perfect ripeness.
Here the only sounds are
Sighs of rain and snow,
Small rustlings of plants
As they unwrap in twilight.
This is where you will go
At last when coldness comes.
It is something you realize
When you first see it,
But instantly forget.
At the end of your life
You remember and dwell in
Its faultless light forever.

# THE GREAT BIRD OF LOVE

I want to become a great night bird
Called The Zimmer, grow intricate gears
And tendons, brace my wings on updrafts,
Roll them down with a motion
That lifts me slowly into the stars
To fly above the troubles of the land.
When I soar the moon will shine past
My shoulder and slide through
Streams like a luminous fish.
I want my cry to be huge and melancholy,
The undefiled movement of my wings
To fold and unfold on rising gloom.

People will see my silhouette from
Their windows and be comforted,
Knowing that, though oppressed,
They are cherished and watched over,
Can turn to kiss their children,
Tuck them into their beds and say:
        Sleep tight.
        No harm tonight,
        In starry skies
        The Zimmer flies.

POETRY FROM ILLINOIS

History Is Your Own Heartbeat
*Michael S. Harper* (1971)

The Foreclosure
*Richard Emil Braun* (1972)

The Scrawny Sonnets and Other
Narratives
*Robert Bagg* (1973)

The Creation Frame
*Phyllis Thompson* (1973)

To All Appearances: Poems New
and Selected
*Josephine Miles* (1974)

The Black Hawk Songs
*Michael Borich* (1975)

Nightmare Begins Responsibility
*Michael S. Harper* (1975)

The Wichita Poems
*Michael Van Walleghen* (1975)

Images of Kin: New and Selected
Poems
*Michael S. Harper* (1977)

Poems of the Two Worlds
*Frederick Morgan* (1977)

Cumberland Station
*Dave Smith* (1977)

Tracking
*Virginia R. Terris* (1977)

Riversongs
*Michael Anania* (1978)

On Earth as It Is
*Dan Masterson* (1978)

Coming to Terms
*Josephine Miles* (1979)

Death Mother and Other Poems
*Frederick Morgan* (1979)

Goshawk, Antelope
*Dave Smith* (1979)

Local Men
*James Whitehead* (1979)

Searching the Drowned Man
*Sydney Lea* (1980)

With Akhmatova at the Black
Gates
*Stephen Berg* (1981)

Dream Flights
*Dave Smith* (1981)

More Trouble with the Obvious
*Michael Van Walleghen* (1981)

The American Book of the Dead
*Jim Barnes* (1982)

The Floating Candles
*Sydnea Lea* (1982)

Northbook
*Frederick Morgan* (1982)

Collected Poems, 1930–83
*Josephine Miles* (1983)

The River Painter
*Emily Grosholz* (1984)

Healing Song for the Inner Ear
*Michael S. Harper* (1984)

Dear John, Dear Coltrane
*Michael S. Harper* (1985)

Poems from the Sangamon
*John Knoepfle* (1985)

Eroding Witness
*Nathaniel Mackey* (1985)
National Poetry Series

In It
*Stephen Berg* (1986)

Palladium
*Alice Fulton* (1986)
National Poetry Series

The Ghosts of Who We Were
*Phyllis Thompson* (1986)

Moon in a Mason Jar
*Robert Wrigley* (1986)

Lower-Class Heresy
*T. R. Hummer* (1987)

Poems: New and Selected
*Frederick Morgan* (1987)

Cities in Motion
*Sylvia Moss* (1987)
National Poetry Series

Furnace Harbor: A
Rhapsody of the North Country
*Philip D. Church* (1988)

The Hand of God and
a Few Bright Flowers
*William Olsen* (1988)
National Poetry Series

Bad Girl, with Hawk
*Nance Van Winckel* (1988)

Blue Tango
*Michael Van Walleghen* (1989)

The Great Bird of Love
*Paul Zimmer* (1989)
National Poetry Series

Eden
*Dennis Schmitz* (1989)